Grades 4–5

Written by Sue O'Connell

Illustrated by Corbin Hillam

Good Apple

A Division of Frank Schaffer Publications, Inc.

Dedication

To Kathy, Dan, Kevin, Joe, and Rita.

Editors: Joanne Corker, Kristin Eclov, Michael Batty
Cover Design: Joanne Caroselli
Book Design: Good Neighbor Press, Inc.

Good Apple
A division of Frank Schaffer Publications, Inc.
23740 Hawthorne Boulevard
Torrance, CA 90505

GA13071

Table of Contents

Rational Numbers (continued)

Statistics/Data Analysis

Probability

Problem Solving

Reflections

Introduction

Why should students write in math class? What does math instruction have to do with writing? What is math journal writing? How do you implement math writing in your busy schedule?

Since the National Council of Teachers of Mathematics (NCTM) Standards began to influence school reform, attention has been directed to the math processes of problem solving, reasoning, communication, and connections—and to how these standards should be evident in all mathematics instruction.

In the past, traditional paper and pencil tasks have required students to fill in the answers. But students need to think, discuss, and write about their mathematics at all grade levels. In the Math—The Write Way series, students write about how they arrive at their answers, justify their mathematical thinking, and describe or define math terms and processes. They are invited to provide real-world examples of math activities and, ultimately, to reflect on their learning. Through this process of constructing answers, students gain a deeper understanding of math concepts and give you a clearer idea of what they know about mathematics.

Consider the following problem:
Which number is larger: 451 or 543?

Here are some ways in which your students might respond:

451 because I'm sure.
Wrong answer; no explanation.

543 because it's bigger.
Correct answer, but does the student understand?

543 because 3 is more than 1.
Correct answer, but the student was comparing ones digits, an incorrect process.

543 because 5 hundreds is more than 4 hundreds.
Correct answer; logical reasoning.

When you ask your students to solve a math problem, they may select the correct response without really understanding the concept. But if you ask them to *explain* the process they used to solve the problem, then they need to demonstrate understanding of the concept in order to complete the task correctly. Written responses require students to have a more thorough knowledge; they also provide insight and information in assessing each student's knowledge and mastery of math concepts and skills.

How Is This Book Organized?

This book is divided into domains based on your mathematics curriculum. These include numeration, whole numbers, rational numbers, geometry, measurement, statistics/data analysis, probability, and problem solving. Each section contains a series of journal pages with writing tasks and activities that coordinate with your math instruction.

The number of activities varies with each domain, since some areas are more strongly emphasized at certain grade levels. These areas lend themselves well to student discussion and writing activities. To facilitate using these activity pages, you will find an answer key at the end of the book.

How Do I Use Journal Pages?

Students need to practice their skills in mathematical communication. These abilities become stronger when students have more opportunities to write about their thinking and to discuss what they've written.

To use the journal pages in this book most effectively, select writing activities that coordinate with the math content and concepts you are teaching in class. You may use these pages throughout the school year as part of your instruction or for assessment. Students can complete the pages in class or as home assignments. You can also pair students to give them opportunities to collaborate and hear how others are thinking. Incorporating writing activities in your math units will provide you with invaluable information to assess your students' knowledge—and help them develop essential math communication skills.

What about Reflections?

The concluding journal pages (Reflections) invite students to reflect on their math learning. Students can use these pages to think about recent lessons—commenting on their understanding of math skills and concepts, verbalizing questions or areas of confusion, and contemplating ways to apply their math skills to real-world situations. You can reuse these pages as students reflect on their learning at various times throughout the year.

By reading your students' reflections, you can gain a great deal of insight into their understanding of mathematics. You may recognize concepts that need to be re-explained, processes that appear confusing, or misunderstandings that are leading to student errors. In addition, you can gain insight into whether students feel competent, frustrated, or satisfied with their math learning. Reviewing student reflection pages can become a valuable tool for assessing your own instructional practices and allow you to modify your lessons based on student feedback.

How Do I Assess Math Writing?

Writing tasks can be scored for both content (the correctness of the response) and communication (the ability to clearly express mathematical ideas). The following rubric can be used to assess students' proficiency in both areas. Student scores can range from 0 to 4 depending on their skill in responding to writing prompts.

Scoring Rubric

4—Information is correct and complete; explanation is clear and contains adequate details

3—Information is correct and complete; explanation may lack clarity or sufficient details

2—Information is partially correct or incomplete; explanation may lack clarity or sufficient details

1—Information is incorrect; explanation is unclear

0—No attempt made

When correcting student-constructed responses, remember that students may explain what they understand in different ways, without using textbook vocabulary or phrasing. Consequently, student responses will vary for many of the activities within this book. When assessing answers, read each response to determine its correctness and use the answer key for suggestions as to what might be included in correct responses.

So go ahead . . . start using the terrific math communication activities throughout this book in your own classroom today and watch your students develop greater confidence, interest, and skill in explaining and exploring mathematics.

Name ____

Round It

Rounding numbers is a helpful math skill. Round each number below to show your rounding skills!

1. Round 4,328 to the nearest hundred. __________

   Explain how you did it.

   ____

   ____

   ____

   ____

   ____

2. Round 6,565 to the nearest thousand. __________

   Explain how you did it.

   ____

   ____

   ____

   ____

   ____

3. Round 23,340 to the nearest thousand. __________

   Explain how you did it.

   ____

   ____

   ____

   ____

   ____

Name ______________________

Numeration

Write It Out

1. Write these numbers in words:

   a. 65,312 ______________________

   b. 436,207,400 ______________________

   c. 2,751,014 ______________________

   d. 750,603 ______________________

   e. 50,381,129 ______________________

   f. 621,473 ______________________

2. Write 621,473 in expanded form.

____

3. Imagine that your friend missed the class when your teacher taught this skill. How would you describe expanded form to your friend?

____

Name ______________________________

Prime or Composite?

You've been asked to do a report for your class on prime and composite numbers. Answer the questions below to help you prepare your report.

1. What is a prime number?

   ____

   ____

   ____

2. Give three examples of prime numbers.

   ____

3. What is a composite number?

   ____

   ____

   ____

4. Give three examples of composite numbers.

   ____

5. Sort the whole numbers from 2 to 20 into the following categories:

Prime	Composite

6. How did you know where to place each number?

   ____

   ____

Name ______________________________

Puzzling Patterns

Professor Pattern prepared these puzzling patterns for you to ponder.

1. Write the next three numbers in the pattern.

   4, 8, 16, 32, ______, ______, ______, . . .

   Describe the pattern. ______________________________

   ____

2. Write the next three numbers in the pattern.

   3, 15, 75, 375, ______, ______, ______, . . .

   Describe the pattern. ______________________________

   ____

3. Write the next three numbers in the pattern.

   2, 5, 9, 14, ______, ______, ______, . . .

   Describe the pattern. ______________________________

   ____

   ____

4. Write a pattern.

   ____

Describe your pattern. ______________________________

____

____

____

____

____

____

____

Name ______________________________

Estimates Are OK

Write a speech to convince your classmates that sometimes an estimate is OK. In your speech, include two examples of times when you need an exact answer. Include two examples of times when an estimate is OK.

Name ______________________________

Multiples and Factors

Connie is confused about multiples and factors. Answer the questions below to help her understand.

1. What is a multiple?

____

____

____

2. List some multiples of 7.

____

____

3. What is a factor?

____

____

____

4. List the factors for 32.

____

____

5. Explain how you know that you listed them all.

____

____

____

____

____

____

____

Name ______________________________

Find the Average

The students at Glenn Dale Elementary celebrated Reading Month with a school Readathon. Some of the students recorded the number of books they read on the table below.

1. What is the average number of books read by the students in the table below?

Books Read for the School Readathon

Student	**Number of Books**
Lisa	16
Kathy	19
Danny	17
Jason	11
Pat	14
Kim	13

Average books read: _______

2. Explain how you found the average number of books read.

____

____

____

____

3. Name a few times when you might need to find an average.

____

____

____

Name ______________________________

Whole Numbers

My Own Story Problems

Create stories to match the number sentences below. Your stories might be about superheroes, snacks, sports, or anything you choose! Be creative!

1. Write a story problem for 325 x 64 = _______.

____

____

____

____

____

Solve your problem.

2. Write a story problem for 564 ÷ 12 = _______.

____

____

____

____

____

Solve your problem.

Name ______________________________

Whole Numbers

Multiplication Mysteries

Can you explain the multiplication mysteries below?

1. Use a picture or diagram to prove that 4 x 6 = 6 x 4.

2. Explain why the product of any number times 0 is 0.

____

____

____

____

3. Does the way in which factors are grouped change the product—for example, (2 x 6) x 4 or 2 x (6 x 4)? Explain your answer.

____

____

____

____

____

____

____

Name ____

Grow a Factor Tree

1. Use a factor tree to find the prime factorization of 50.

2. How can a factor tree help you determine if a number is prime or composite?

____

____

____

____

____

____

3. Is it true that the larger a number is, the more factors it has? Give examples to justify your answer.

____

____

____

____

____

____

____

Name ______________________________

Exponents and Factors

1. Use a factor tree to find the prime factorization of 64.

2. Explain how an exponent can help you name the prime factors of a number. Use the prime factors of 6^4 as an example.

____

____

____

____

3. What does 2^3 mean?

____

____

____

____

4. Name the value of $3^2 \times 2^3$. Explain how you got your answer.

____

____

____

____

Name ____

ASAP, Find the GCF and LCM!

Confused Connie needs your help! Can you help her understand what greatest common factors and least common multiples are?

1. What is a greatest common factor (GCF)?

   ____

   ____

2. What is the greatest common factor of 24 and 32? _______

   Explain how you found it.

   ____

   ____

   ____

3. Find the GCFs for these numbers.

   18, 24 ________ 15, 20 ________ 12, 30 ________

4. What is a least common multiple (LCM)?

   ____

   ____

5. What is the LCM of 9 and 6? _______ Explain how you found it.

   ____

   ____

   ____

6. Find the LCM for these numbers.

   6 ,8 ________ 12, 10 ________ 5, 6 ________

Name ______________________________

What's Happening?

1. Look at the table below. Complete the table.

In	Out
1	3
2	6
3	9
4	

Write the rule that explains what is happening in the table.

____

____

2. Look at the table below. Complete the table.

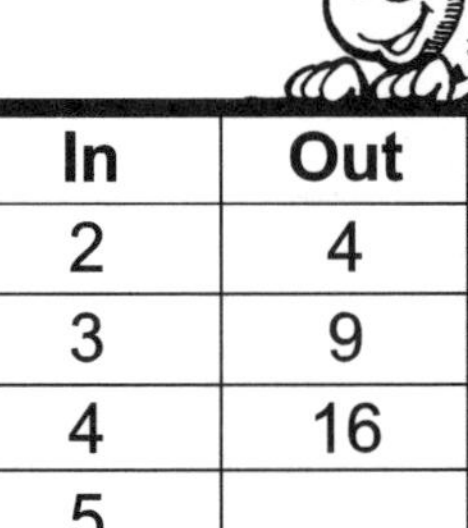

In	Out
2	4
3	9
4	16
5	

Write the rule that explains what is happening in the table.

____

____

3. Create a table.

In	Out

Write the rule for the table.

____

____

____

Name ____

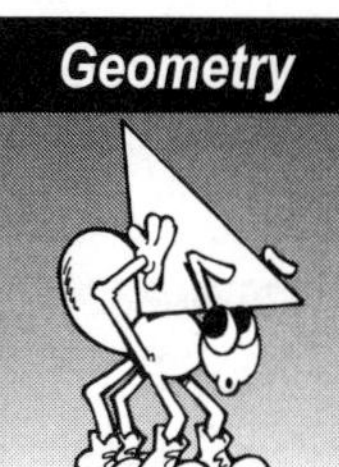

Three Terrific Triangles

1. Describe an isosceles, an equilateral, and a scalene triangle.

   Isosceles:

   ____

   ____

   ____

   Equilateral:

   ____

   ____

   ____

   Scalene:

   ____

   ____

   ____

2. Draw and label a picture of each type of triangle.

Name ____________________

Circle Talk

1. Help someone understand a circle by using the words in the Word Bank in your description.

2. Draw a diagram that explains the words.

3. What is the relationship between the radius and the diameter of a circle?

4. Is the diameter also a chord? Justify your answer.

Name ____

Similar or Congruent?

Imagine that you are the teacher. Help your class understand similar and congruent figures.

1. Compare and contrast similar and congruent figures.

____
____
____
____
____
____
____
____

2. Draw and label a diagram to help explain the two.

Name ______________________________

What's Your Angle?

1. Explain the terms *acute angle, obtuse angle*, and *right angle*.

   Acute angle:

   ____

   ____

   ____

   Obtuse angle:

   ____

   ____

   ____

   Right angle:

   ____

   ____

   ____

2. Draw and label an example of each.

Name ______________________________

All About Angles

1. Draw an angle that is more than 90 degrees and an angle that is less than 90 degrees. Label your pictures.

2. How do you know that an angle is more than 90 degrees without measuring it?

____

____

____

3. What tool will you use to measure the angles below? ______________

4. Measure the angles and record each measurement.

Angle 1 __________ Angle 2 __________

5. Notice that there are two numbers you must choose from to determine the angle measurement. How did you know which number was correct? Explain.

____

____

____

____

Name ______________________________

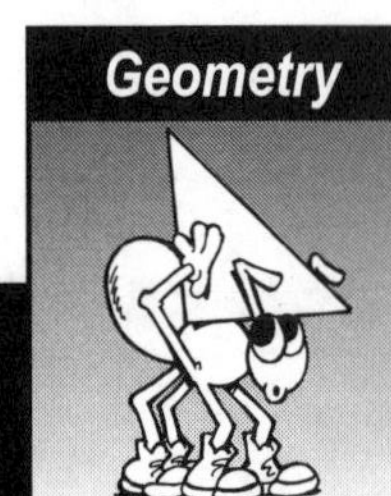

Six Solid Shapes

1. Fill in each blank with a number.

Triangular prism

_____ flat faces

_____ edges

_____ vertices

Square pyramid

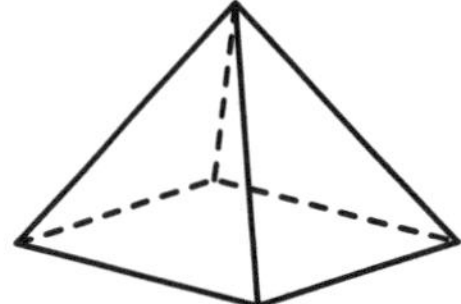

_____ flat faces

_____ edges

_____ vertices

2. Describe the characteristics of a rectangular prism. Use the words *edges, faces,* and *vertices*.

Rectangular prism

____

____

____

____

3. Describe the characteristics of a cylinder. Use the words *edges* and *faces* in your description.

Cylinder

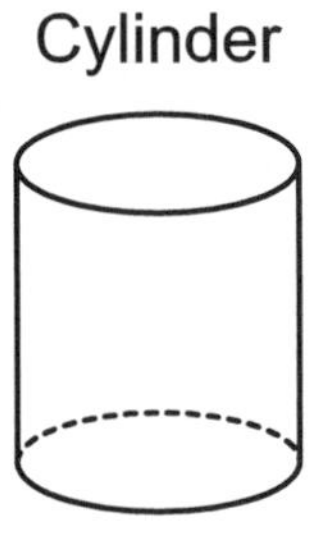

____

____

____

____

4. Name real-world examples of the following shapes: cylinder, sphere, rectangular prism, and cone.

____

____

____

____

Name ______________________________

Symmetry

1. Does this polygon have a line of symmetry? Explain. If there is a line of symmetry, draw it on the figure.

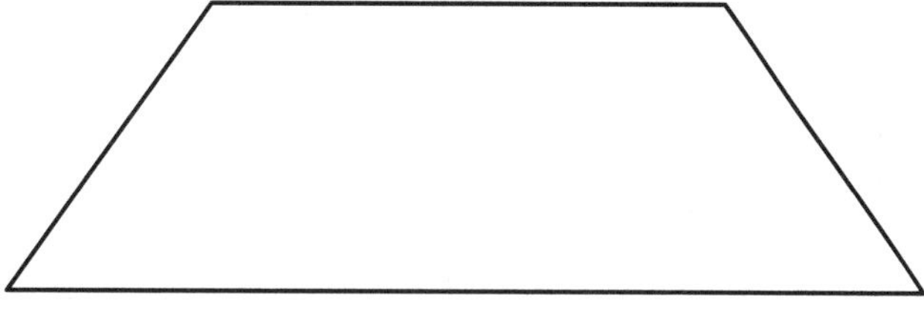

2. Does this polygon have a line of symmetry? Explain. If there is a line of symmetry, draw it on the figure.

3. Which letters in your first and last names have lines of symmetry? Draw the letters and draw the line of symmetry through each.

Name ________________________________

How Much Should You Buy?

Your class is planning an egg hunt for the first graders.

1. If you need 65 eggs for the hunt, how many dozen should you buy? ____________

How do you know?

____

____

____

____

2. You will need to buy ribbon to decorate the prize basket. The ribbon is sold by the yard. How many yards should you buy if you need $10\frac{1}{2}$ feet of ribbon? __________

Explain.

____

____

____

____

Name ____________________

Nearest Dollar

Erica was shopping for groceries. As she picked up each item, she rounded the price to the nearest dollar so that she could keep track of about how much money she would pay.

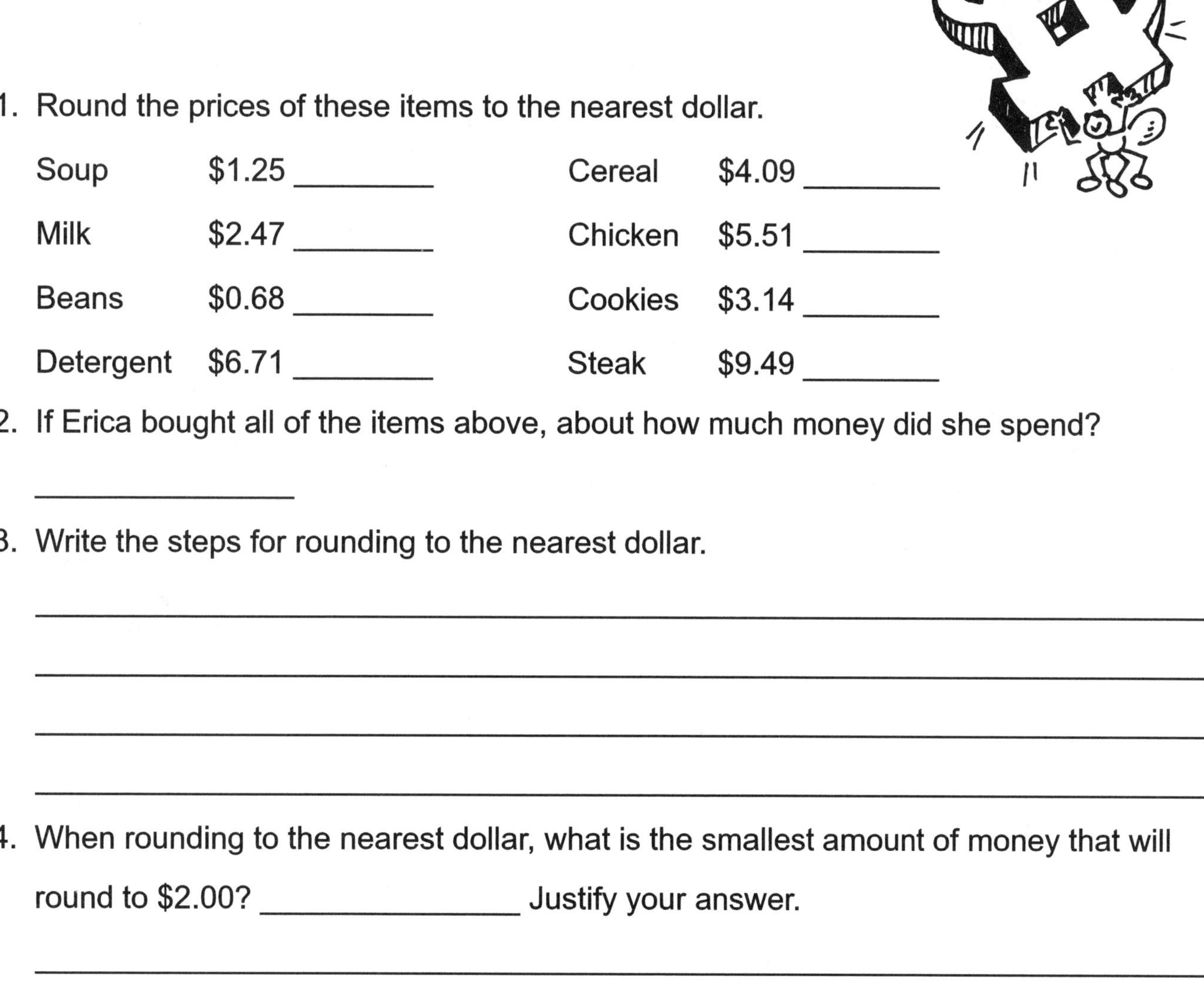

1. Round the prices of these items to the nearest dollar.

Soup	$1.25	________	Cereal	$4.09	________
Milk	$2.47	________	Chicken	$5.51	________
Beans	$0.68	________	Cookies	$3.14	________
Detergent	$6.71	________	Steak	$9.49	________

2. If Erica bought all of the items above, about how much money did she spend?

   ____

3. Write the steps for rounding to the nearest dollar.

   ____

   ____

   ____

   ____

4. When rounding to the nearest dollar, what is the smallest amount of money that will round to $2.00? ______________ Justify your answer.

   ____

   ____

   ____

   ____

Name ______________________________

Measurement

Coin Combinations

Brendan doesn't like to carry a lot of coins in his pocket. For each item below, what coins should he use to pay with the fewest possible?

1. Gum 27¢

   ____

   Prove your answer.

   ____

   ____

2. Candy 46¢

   ____

3. Soft drink 68¢

   ____

4. Cupcake 82¢

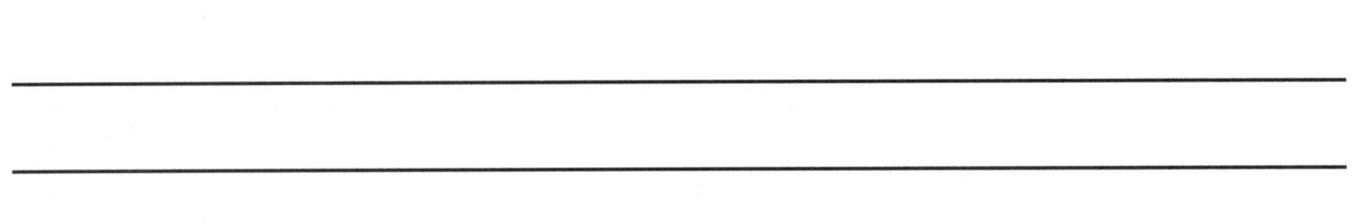

5. Trading cards $1.96

   ____

6. Think about how you solved each problem above. Write a tip for finding the fewest coins to make a given amount.

   ____

   ____

Name ________________________________

Sleeping or Studying?

Do you spend more time in bed, or at school?

1. Estimate the number of hours you spend sleeping during a typical week.

   ____

   Explain how you made your estimate.

   ____

   ____

   ____

2. What additional information will you need to solve this problem:
   In a typical week, do you spend more hours sleeping, or in school?

   ____

   ____

   ____

3. Solve the problem here.

   I spend more time ____________________.

   Does your answer surprise you? Why, or why not?

   ____

   ____

   ____

Name ______________________________

Inside and Around

1. Define *area* and explain how you find the area of a rectangle.

2. Define *perimeter*. Explain how you find the perimeter of a rectangle.

3. If two figures both have an area of 24 square units, do they always have the same perimeter? Justify your answer.

4. Why is area measured in square units?

Name ____________________

Measurement

Picnic Problem

You and five of your friends are having a picnic and want to divide the food evenly. Look at the food list and decide how much of each item should be given to each person.

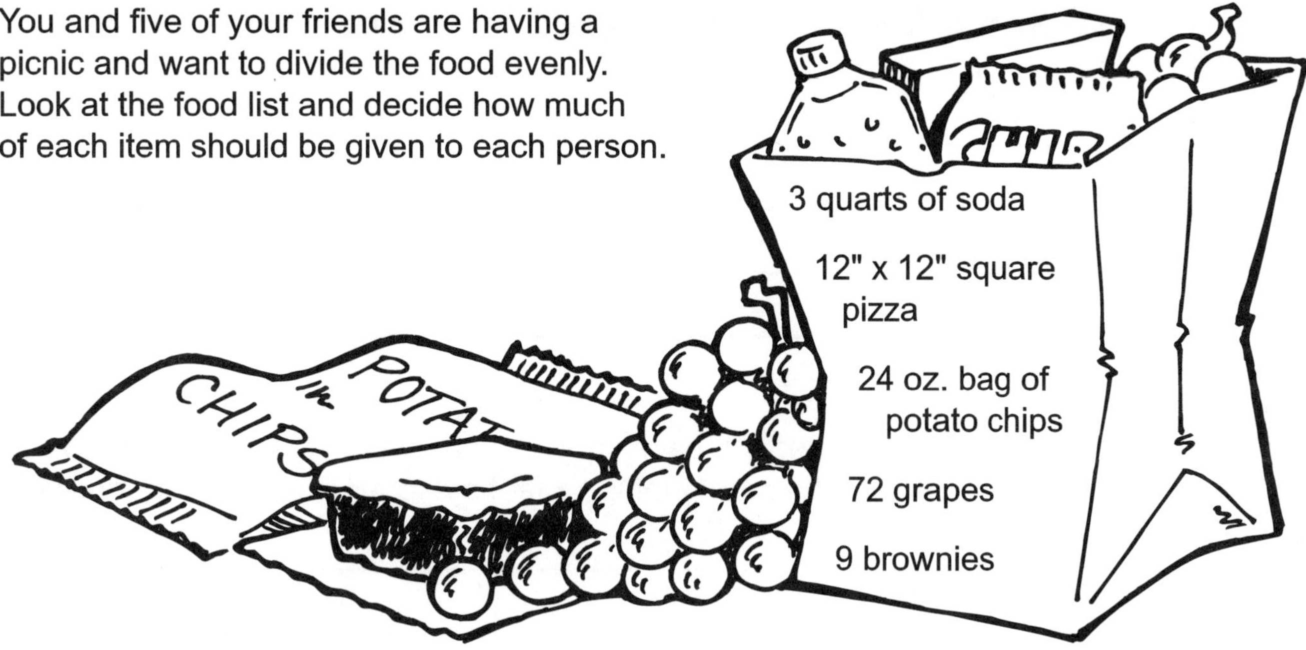

1. Write your plan for sharing the food below.

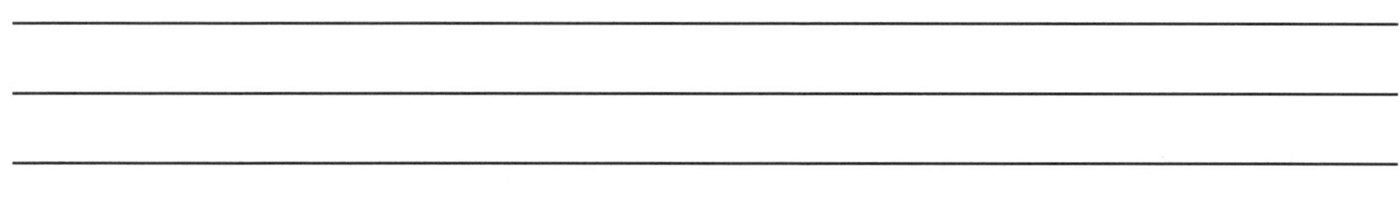

2. Prove that your way of sharing is a fair one.

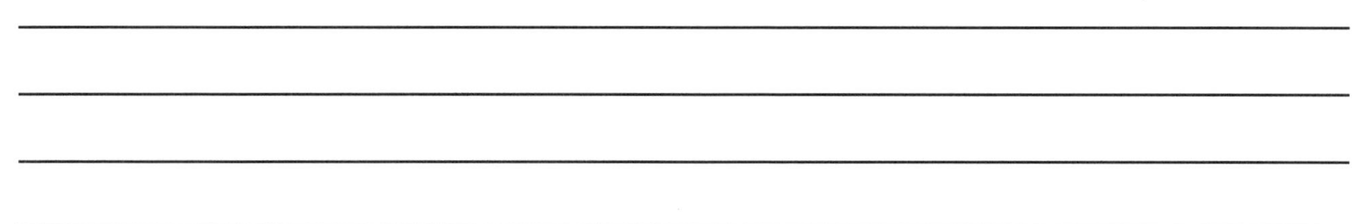

Name ______________________________

Do You Have Enough?

1. If you have 80 yards of fence, do you have enough to surround a kennel that is 25 yards by 20 yards? Explain.

____

____

____

____

____

2. If you have 200 squares of carpet and each square measures one square foot, do you have enough squares to carpet a room that is 12 feet by 15 feet? Justify your answer.

____

____

____

____

____

3. If you have 100 square feet of carpet, do you have enough to carpet this room? Justify your answer.

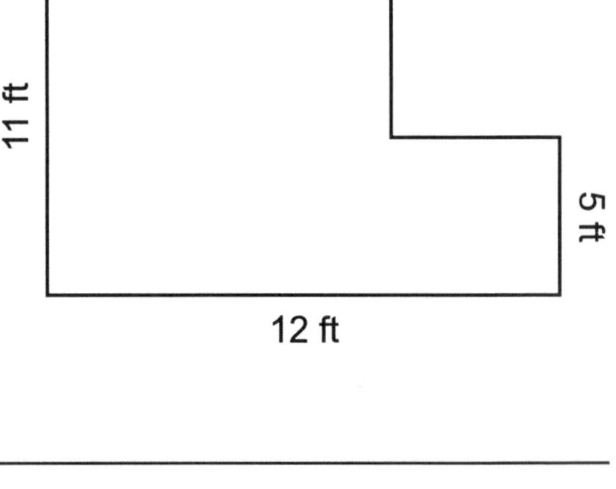

____

____

____

Name ______________________________

Time to Swim

Use what you know about elapsed time to answer the questions below.

1. It was 2:30 p.m. when Rita began her swimming lesson. The lesson lasted 45 minutes. When did the lesson end? Explain your answer.

____

____

____

2. After her lesson, Rita stayed at the pool to swim with her friends until her mother came to get her at 4:40 p.m. How much time did she get to swim with her friends? Explain your answer.

____

____

____

3. It took Rita 10 minutes to get changed and 15 minutes to ride home. At what time did she get home? Justify your answer.

____

____

____

4. Add one more part to this problem.

____

____

____

____

____

____

Write the answer to your problem. ______________

Name ____________________

Fraction Action

Show what you know about fractions by illustrating each fraction in the boxes below. Write a phrase to explain each drawing.

$\frac{1}{6}$ ____________________ ____________________	$\frac{1}{4}$ ____________________ ____________________
$\frac{5}{3}$ ____________________ ____________________	$\frac{4}{4}$ ____________________ ____________________

Reproducible

Name ______________________________

Fishy Fractions

Mrs. Pescadore's class went on a field trip to the aquarium. Use what you know about fractions to answer these questions about the trip.

1. Two-thirds of the students went to the shark exhibit as soon as they arrived at the aquarium. There were 24 students in the class. How many students visited the shark exhibit first? ________
   Explain how you got your answer.

   ____

   ____

   ____

   ____

2. Solve the following problems to find out the students' favorite aquarium resident.

   a. $\frac{1}{2}$ of 16 = ________

   b. $\frac{4}{6}$ of 18 = ________

   c. $\frac{4}{5}$ of 20 = ________

   d. $\frac{3}{5}$ of 15 = ________

   e. $\frac{1}{4}$ of 16 = ________

   f. $\frac{2}{3}$ of 21 = ________

   g. $\frac{5}{6}$ of 18 = ________

3. To solve the puzzle, convert each answer to a letter of the alphabet (1 = A, 2 = B, 3 = C, 4 = D, and so on). Then unscramble the letters.

   ____

Name ____

Equivalent Fractions

Your teacher says that understanding equivalent fractions is very important.

1. What is an equivalent fraction?

____

____

____

____

____

____

____

____

2. Write two equivalent fractions for $\frac{2}{3}$. _____, _____
3. Write two equivalent fractions for $\frac{4}{5}$. _____, _____
4. Convince your teacher that you understand how to find an equivalent fraction by writing the directions for finding one for $\frac{3}{5}$.

____

____

____

____

____

____

____

____

Name ____

Sale!

1. The store is having a half-off sale. Calculate the sale price for each item.

Gigantic Sale! • Everything $\frac{1}{2}$ Off!

Shirt	$22.50	Sale price: __________!
Jeans	$35.00	Sale price: __________!
Gloves	$ 9.00	Sale price: __________!
Hat	$12.60	Sale price: __________!
Sandals	$15.70	Sale price: __________!
Athletic shoes	$36.40	Sale price: __________!

2. Explain how you found the sale price.

____

____

3. Pick three items to buy. Explain what you will buy and what the total cost of your purchases will be.

____

____

Challenge: The store charges 5% tax on your purchase. How much will your total bill be, including tax? Explain how you figured this out.

____

____

Name ______________________________

Adding Fractions

Your friend was absent when the teacher explained adding fractions. Answer the questions below to help your friend understand.

1. Solve these problems:

a. $\frac{4}{9} + \frac{2}{9} =$ ______

c. $\frac{1}{4} + \frac{5}{12} =$ ______

b. $\frac{2}{7} + \frac{4}{21} =$ ______

d. $\frac{2}{18} + \frac{1}{6} =$ ______

2. Write the steps you need to follow to add fractions with like denominators.

____

____

____

____

____

____

3. How would your directions be different if they showed how to add fractions with unlike denominators? Write the new directions.

____

____

____

____

____

____

____

____

Name ____________________

Convince Me

Your friend thinks that fractions are useless. Write a letter to this friend to convince him or her that fractions are important. Use examples to help your friend understand.

Name ______________________________

It's Just Not Proper!

Some fractions look different than others!

1. What is an improper fraction?

____

____

____

____

____

____

2. Convert these improper fractions to mixed numbers.

a. $\frac{12}{7}$ __________

b. $\frac{14}{6}$ __________

c. $\frac{21}{8}$ __________

d. $\frac{15}{4}$ __________

e. $\frac{25}{6}$ __________

3. Write the steps you follow to convert an improper fraction to a mixed number.

____

____

____

____

____

____

Name ____

Ready, Set, Reduce!

Your classmates are learning how to reduce fractions. Check their work below.

1. Jonathan reduced $\frac{6}{10}$ to $\frac{2}{5}$. Was he correct? Why or why not?

____

____

____

____

2. Amanda reduced $\frac{6}{9}$ to $\frac{2}{3}$. Was she correct? Why or why not?

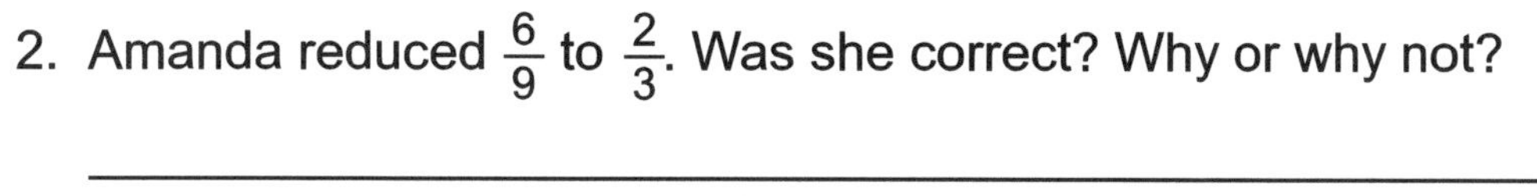

____

____

____

____

3. Reduce these fractions to lowest terms.

a. $\frac{3}{9}$ = ________

d. $\frac{6}{15}$ = ________

b. $\frac{4}{16}$ = ________

e. $\frac{15}{20}$ = ________

c. $\frac{4}{8}$ = ________

f. $\frac{15}{25}$ = ________

4. Explain how to reduce $\frac{4}{24}$ to lowest terms.

____

____

____

____

Name ____

Decimal Patterns

Professor Pattern has some decimal patterns for you to ponder.

1. Write the next three numbers in the following pattern:

   2.1, 2.7, 3.3, 3.9, _____, _____, _____, . . .

   Describe the pattern.

   ____

   ____

2. Write the next three numbers in the following pattern:

   3, 4.5, 6, 7.5, _____, _____, _____, . . .

   Describe the pattern.

   ____

   ____

3. Write the next three numbers in the following pattern:

   4.53, 4.55, 4.57, 4.59, _____, _____, _____, . . .

   Describe the pattern.

   ____

   ____

4. Write a decimal pattern.

   ____

   Describe your pattern.

   ____

   ____

Name ______________________________

Round the Jumps

1. Yorktown School had a Track and Field Day. The table below shows the distance jumped by each student in a standing broad jump contest. The rules say that all scores should first be rounded to the nearest whole number, and then the distances should be ordered from the longest jump to the shortest to determine the winner. Round each score to the nearest whole number.

Student	***Distance jumped (in cm)***	***Rounded to whole number***
Jean	*65.6*	
Pat	*75.3*	
Terrell	*62.4*	
Bobby	*83.9*	
Kathleen	*83.2*	
Carol	*69.6*	
Carlos	*71.7*	
Michael	*71.5*	

2. How might you decide who wins any ties?

____

____

3. The order from first to last is

a. ______________ e. ______________

b. ______________ f. ______________

c. ______________ g. ______________

d. ______________ h. ______________

4. Explain how to round decimals to the nearest whole number.

____

____

Name ____

Same Number, Different Name

1. Write the following fractions as decimals and in words:

Fraction	*Decimal*	*Words*
$\frac{4}{10}$	*0.4*	*four tenths*
$\frac{32}{100}$		
$\frac{6}{10}$		
$\frac{53}{100}$		
$\frac{7}{100}$		

2. Use words or drawings to convince someone that 0.5 = 0.50.

____

____

____

____

____

____

Name ____

Tricky Tenths and Hundredths

Decimal Dan is trying to trick you! Use what you know about decimals to outsmart him.

1. Which decimal is greater—2.08 or 2.14? Explain your answer.

2. Which decimal is greater—7.05 or 7.5? Explain your answer.

3. Order the following decimals from least to greatest:
   2.04, 2.8, 2.08, 2.48, 2.84.

4. Write a tip for someone who might be unsure of how to order decimals.

Name ______________________________

Percents to Ponder

1. What is a percent?

____

____

____

____

2. There were 50 jelly beans in the jar. 10% of them were green. How many green jelly beans were in the jar? __________

   Explain how you got your answer.

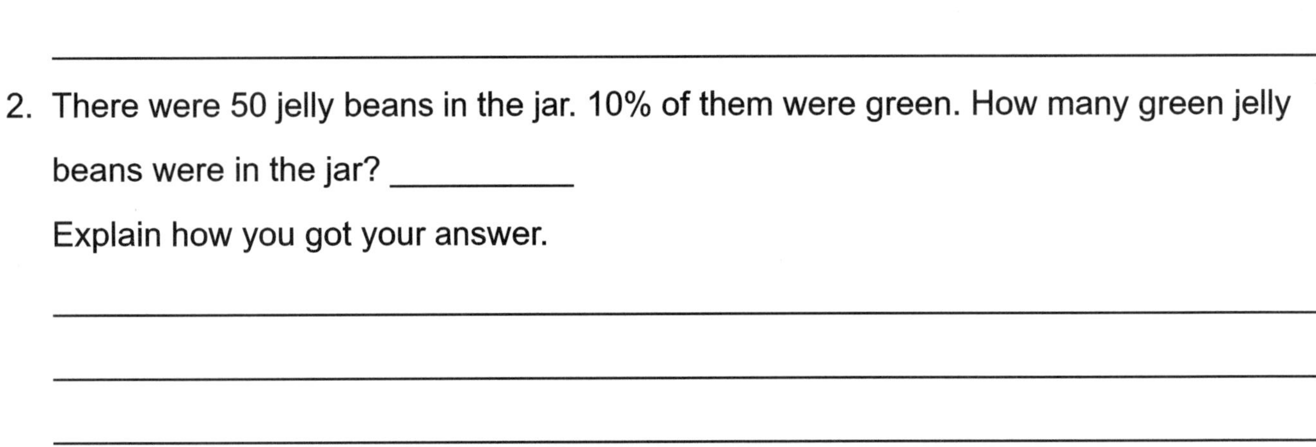

3. Solve the following:

   a. 10% of 70 = __________

   b. 50% of 80 = __________

   c. 20% of 60 = __________

   d. 10% of 90 = __________

   e. 20% of 200 = __________

4. When might you use a percent?

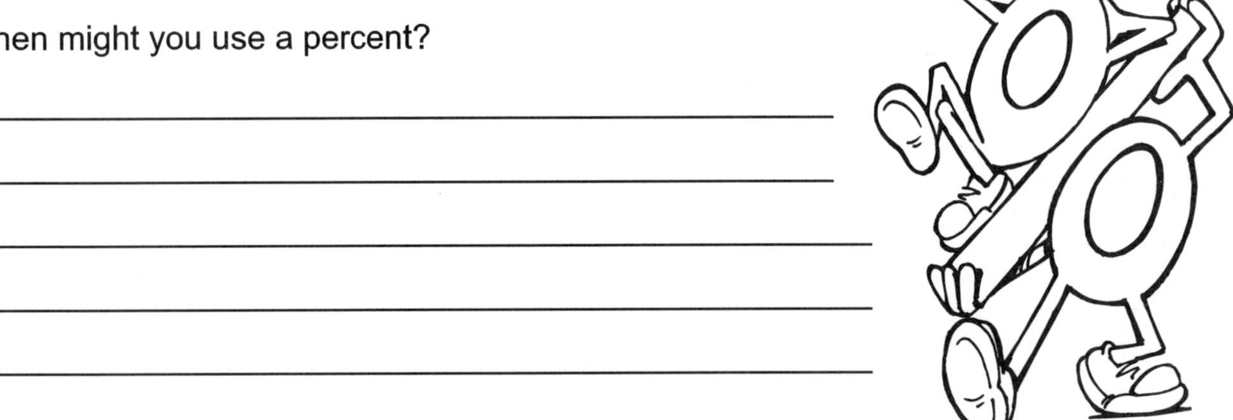

Name ____

The Best Graph

1. Which type of graph would you use to display data about rainfall during the month of April? Why?

____

____

____

____

2. Which type of graph would you use to display data about your classmates' favorite types of cookies? Why?

____

____

____

____

3. Which type of graph would you use to display data about the heights of five of the world's tallest mountains? Why?

____

____

____

____

4. Give an example of data that would best be displayed by using a double bar graph. Justify your answer.

____

____

____

____

Name ______________________________

Diving Data

1. You have been asked to help the judges in a diving competition. There are seven judges. Each judge rates a dive from 0 (worst) to 10 (best). Find each diver's final score by using the competition scoring rules.

> Scoring rules: The high score and the low score are thrown out, and then the other five scores are averaged.

Erica	7.8,	6.5,	6.9,	7.9,	8.2,	8.3,	7.7
Colleen	7.8,	9.2,	8.9,	8.8,	7.9,	8.6,	7.8
Rita	9.3,	9.1,	8.3,	7.4,	7.6,	8.4,	8.1
Megan	7.9,	8.0,	7.5,	7.7,	7.5,	9.1,	8.4
Melissa	8.8,	9.0,	8.8,	7.9,	7.8,	8.3,	8.7

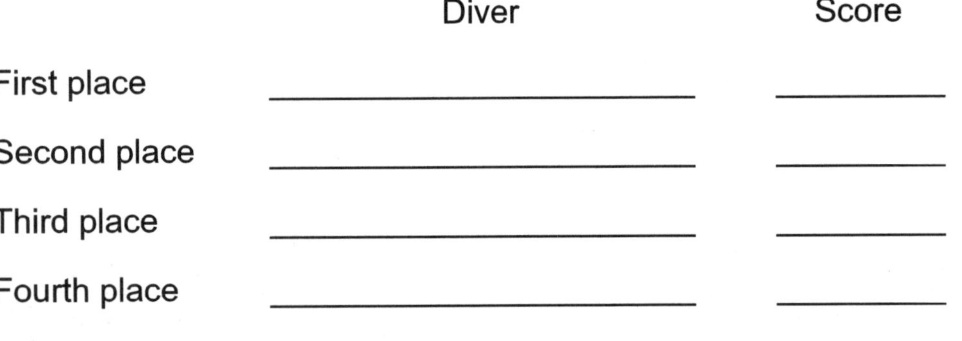

	Diver	Score
First place	____________	______
Second place	____________	______
Third place	____________	______
Fourth place	____________	______
Fifth place	____________	______

2. If you threw out the high and low scores and selected the winner based on the median score, would the same person win? Justify your answer.

____

____

____

____

Name ______________________________

Flavor Graph

1. Look at the data table for Super Scoops Ice Cream Shop. Table 1 shows the amount of ice cream sold by flavor. Design a graph to show the data.

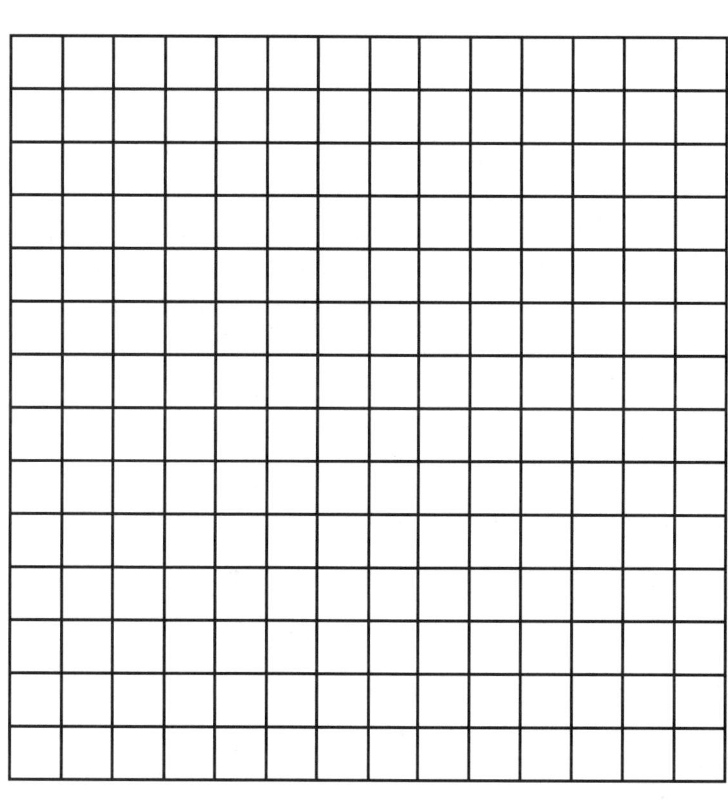

TABLE 1

Flavor	Amount sold today
Chocolate	52 gallons
Vanilla	49 gallons
Chocolate chip	68 gallons
Butter pecan	35 gallons
Fudge swirl	48 gallons
Orange sherbet	25 gallons
Lime sherbet	16 gallons

2. Which type of graph did you choose, and why?

____

____

3. What conclusions can you draw from this graph?

____

____

4. For what might the owner of the ice cream shop use the information on this graph?

____

____

Name ____________________

Ice Cream by the Hour

1. Table 2 shows the amount of ice cream sold each hour throughout the day at Super Scoops Ice Cream Shop. Design a graph to show the data.

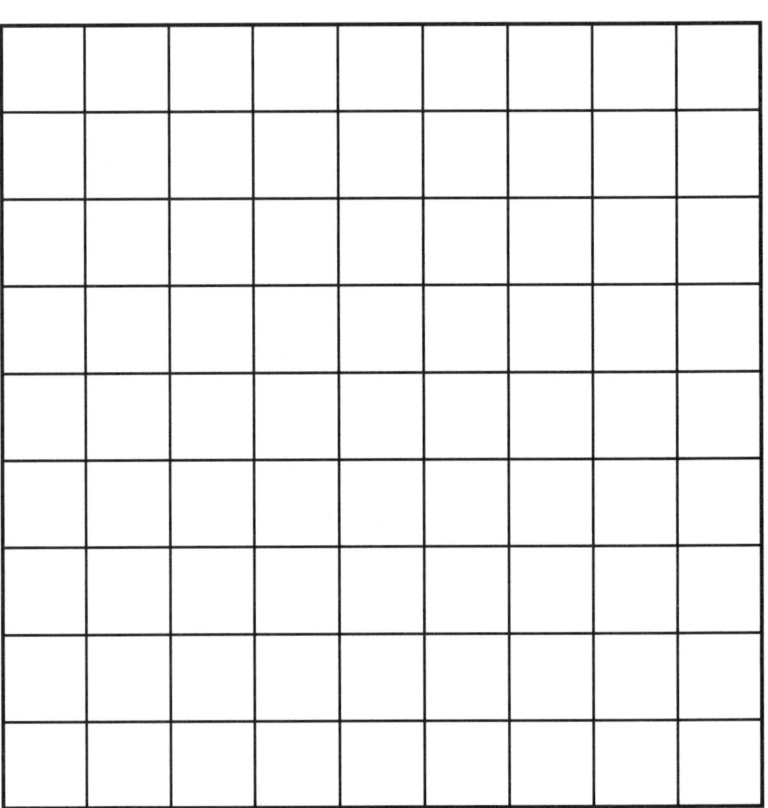

TABLE 2

Hour of day	Gallons sold
11:00 a.m.–noon	6 gallons
Noon–1:00 p.m.	9 gallons
1:00–2:00 p.m.	15 gallons
2:00–3:00 p.m.	30 gallons
3:00–4:00 p.m.	35 gallons
4:00–5:00 p.m.	40 gallons
5:00–6:00 p.m.	33 gallons
6:00–7:00 p.m.	57 gallons
7:00–8:00 p.m.	68 gallons

2. Which type of graph did you choose, and why?

____

____

3. Why might the information on this graph be helpful to the owner of the ice cream shop?

____

____

Name ______________________________

Statistics/Data Analysis

Favorite Cereals

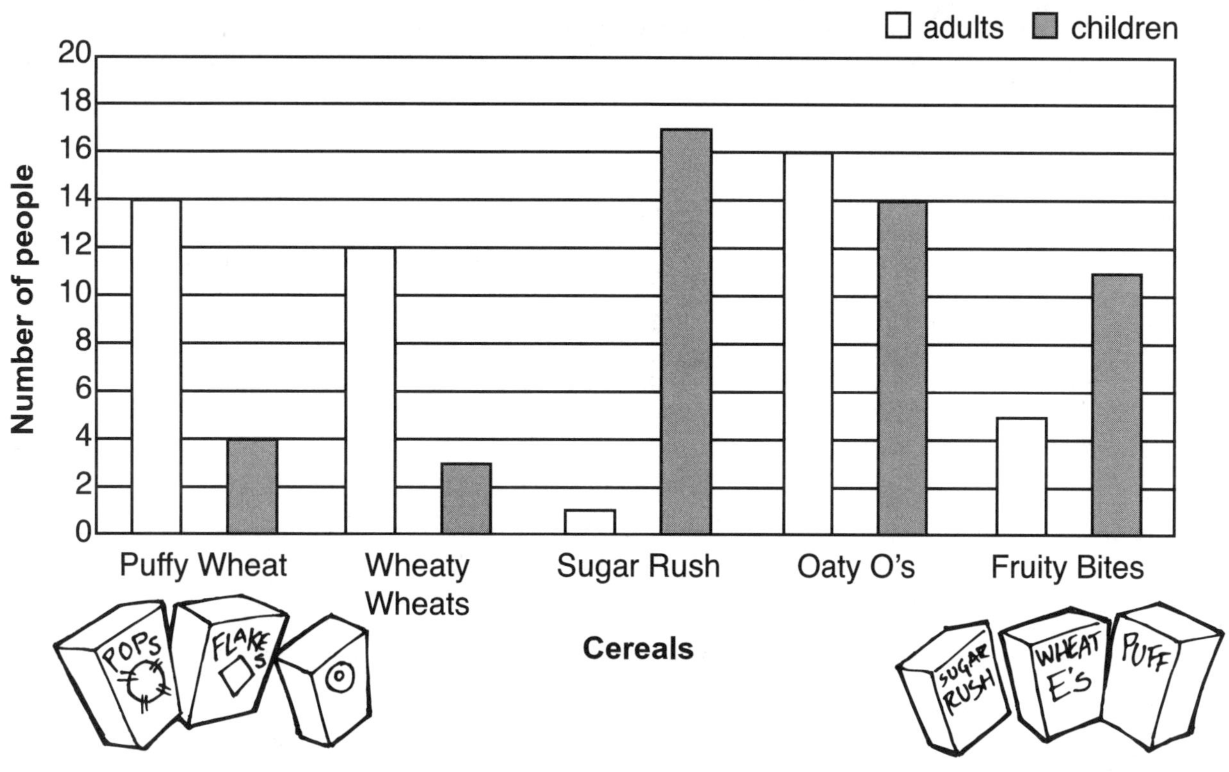

1. What does this double bar graph show?

____

____

2. Write three facts you've learned from the graph.

____

____

____

3. Does the data on the graph surprise you? Why, or why not?

____

____

4. Who might be interested in this data? Why?

____

____

Name ______________________________

Carnival Coupons

1. At the school carnival, the children won coupons at each game. The coupons could be redeemed for prizes at the prize booth. Set up a line plot to show the number of coupons won by each child.

Joe	4	Allison	1	Melissa	8
Christopher	5	Celeste	8	Kevin	5
Laura	2	Kim	6	Mark	8
Dave	9	Katie	8	Michele	6

1 2 3 4 5 6 7 8 9 10

2. What was the greatest number of coupons won? __________

3. What was the least number of coupons won? __________

4. What is the range? ____________

   Explain how you know.

   ____

   ____

   ____

5. What is the mode? ____________

   Explain how you know.

   ____

   ____

   ____

Name ____

Sweet Sales

The stem and leaf plot at the right shows the number of boxes of candy sold by each class for the school fund-raiser.

Boxes of Candy Sold by Each Class

Stems	Leaves
4	0,2,7,8,9
5	0,0,2,2,2,4,4,5,7
6	0,1

1. What was the greatest amount of candy sold by a class? Explain how you know.

____

____

2. What was the least amount of candy sold by a class? Explain how you know.

____

____

3. Each class sold about how many boxes? (Look at the plot to estimate the average number sold by each class.) ______________ Explain why you chose this number as your estimate.

____

____

4. How many classes were in the school? Explain how you know.

____

____

5. How many classes sold at least 50 boxes? Explain how you know.

____

____

____

Name ______________________________

Bicycle Prices

The table below shows the prices of bicycles at Bubby's Bike Shop. Let's explore mean, median, mode, and range by using the bicycle data.

Bicycle	Cost
Blazer	$129
Stealth	$ 99
Speedster	$115
Champion	$ 94
Rocket	$125
Speed Demon	$121
Stallion	$115

1. What is the range of prices for the bicycles? ______________

   Explain what a range is and how you figure it out.

   ____

   ____

2. What is the mean cost for a bicycle? ______________

3. What is the median cost? ______________

   Explain the difference between a mean and a median.

   ____

   ____

   ____

4. What is a mode, and how do you find it?

   ____

   ____

5. What is the mode for this data? ______________

Name ____

A Tree-mendous Diagram

Tree diagrams can help you organize your ideas.

1. Create a tree diagram to show the outcomes for flipping two coins.

2. Set up a tree diagram to show all choices for selecting a skateboard that could be made of wood or acrylic and colored blue, red, silver, or black.

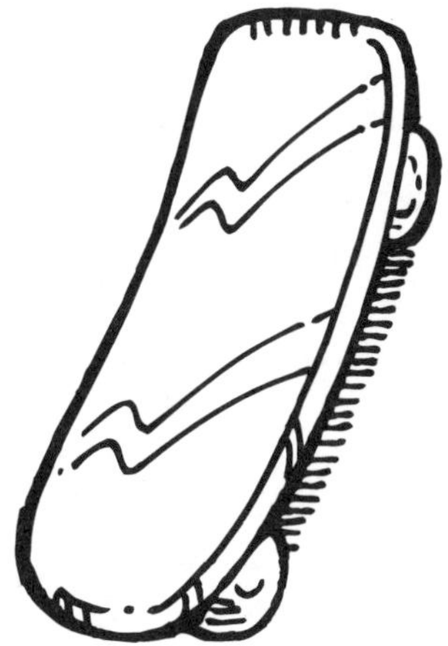

3. Explain how a tree diagram helps you list all possible outcomes of an event.

____

____

____

____

Name ______________________________

Equally Likely?

It is likely that you will read something today. It is unlikely that you will win $1,000 before dinner.

1. Give examples of outcomes that are equally likely.

2. Give examples of outcomes that are not equally likely.

3. Define *equally likely*.

Name ____

Roll the Die

1. What is the probability of rolling a 3 when you roll a die? ________

   Explain your answer.

   ____
   ____
   ____
   ____
   ____

2. What is the probability of rolling a number less than 3? ________

   Explain your answer.

   ____
   ____
   ____
   ____

3. What is the probability of rolling a number greater than 3? ________

   Explain your answer.

   ____
   ____
   ____
   ____

4. What are some real-world examples of times when you might use probability?

   ____
   ____
   ____
   ____

Name ______________________________

Marble Probability

Katie has a bag containing the following colors of marbles: 4 green, 2 red, 2 blue, 1 yellow, and 1 orange.

1. If she pulls one marble out of the bag, how many different color outcomes are possible? ______________

2. Which color is she most likely to pick? ______________

   Explain your answer.

   ____

   ____

   ____

3. Which color is she least likely to pick? ______________

   Explain your answer.

   ____

   ____

   ____

4. What would be an impossible outcome? ______________

   Explain your answer.

   ____

   ____

   ____

5. Does the most likely outcome always occur when doing a probability experiment?

   Explain your answer.

   ____

   ____

   ____

Name ____

Problem Solving

What's Your Strategy?

1. Kevin is helping his father fence in a part of the yard for their dog. The area they are fencing in is 25 feet wide and 15 feet long. They need a post in the ground every 5 feet.

   How many posts will they need? ________________

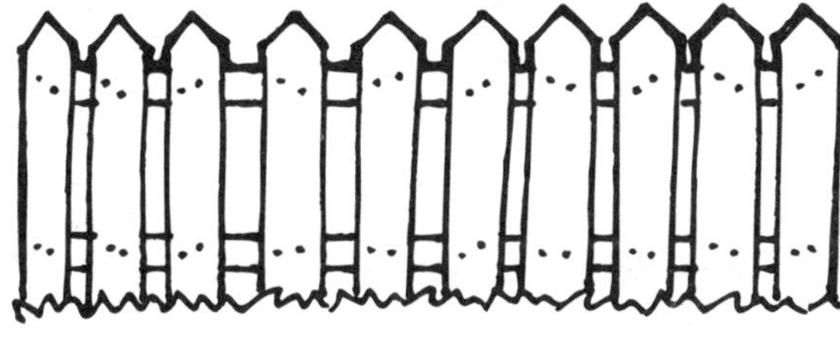

   Explain the strategy you used to solve this problem.

   ____
   ____
   ____
   ____

2. Joseph had 24 baseball cards. He sorted them into two categories—American League and National League players. He had 6 more American League than National League.

   How many of each did he have? ________________

   Explain how you solved this problem.

   ____
   ____
   ____
   ____

Name ____

Problem Solving

Playground Favorites

Gail, José, Kelly, and Maria each have a favorite playground game. They like jump rope, tag, basketball, and kickball. José does not like to kick the ball. Maria loves to play tag. Kelly hates to jump rope. Gail's game is played with a ball. Kelly bounces the ball when she plays.

1. Which playground game is each child's favorite? Use the matrix to help you organize your clues and solve the problem.

Gail				
José				
Kelly				
Maria				

2. How did using a matrix help you solve the problem?

____

____

____

____

____

____

____

____

Name ______________________________

Problem Solving

Muffins Enough

Susie loves Cinnamon Chip Muffins! She wants to make enough muffins for the 28 students in her class.

1. How many batches (recipes) will she need to make? Explain.

____

____

2. How much of each ingredient will she need?

Cinnamon Chip Muffins

	Amount needed
2 cups flour	____________
$\frac{1}{4}$ cup sugar	____________
1 egg	____________
$\frac{2}{3}$ cup milk	____________
1 cup chocolate chips	____________
$\frac{1}{3}$ cup chopped nuts	____________
$\frac{1}{2}$ teaspoon cinnamon sugar	____________

Makes about 12 muffins.

3. Explain how you figured this out.

____

____

4. Write a problem that can be solved by using the data from the recipe.

____

____

5. Solve your problem.

____

Name ______________________________

Problem Solving

Please Explain

1. There were twenty-seven students in Mrs. Higgins' class. Sixteen students were wearing red. Nineteen students were wearing blue. Every student was wearing at least one of the two colors. How many students were wearing both red and blue?

   ____

   What strategy did you use to solve this?

   ____

   ____

   ____

   ____

2. Kim went to the store to buy gifts for her family. First she spent half of her money on a gift for her mother. Then she spent $10.50 on a gift for her father. Next she spent $9.75 on a gift for her sister. She had $12.50 left. How much did she have at the start?

   ____

   Explain how you got your answer.

   ____

   ____

   ____

   ____

Name ______________________________

Problem Solving

What a Racket!

Tennis racket	$ 27.96
Racket case	$ 13.47
Tennis balls	$ 2.75
Water bottle	$ 2.18
Tennis shoes	$ 32.50

Tennis Bargain Pack

(Racket, case, and balls) **$39.95**

1. How much will it cost to buy a tennis racket and three cans of tennis balls? Explain how you got your answer.

____

____

2. Is the Tennis Bargain Pack a good deal? Justify your answer.

____

____

____

3. If you wanted to buy all five items (racket, case, balls, bottle, and shoes), how much would it cost? Find the cheapest way to buy all five.

Explain why this is the cheapest way.

____

____

____

Name ______________________________

Problem Solving

The Riddler

1. Guess my number.
   It is greater than 20.
   It is less than 40.
   It is a multiple of 6.
   The sum of its digits is 9.

   My number is ________ .

2. Guess my number.
   It is a multiple of 3.
   It is less than 30.
   It is a two-digit number.
   One of its digits is a 2.
   It is a multiple of 7.

   My number is ________ .

3. Guess my number.
   It is less than 50.
   It is a multiple of 9.
   It is a two-digit number.
   The difference between the two digits is 5.

   My number is ________ .

4. Give two tips for solving these riddles.

____

____

____

5. Make up a number riddle of your own.

____

____

____

6. Solve your riddle.

____

Name ____

Problem Solving

Color Combos

The Bowie Bucks baseball team is selecting new uniforms. Help them solve the following problems so they can decide which colors to choose.

1. They have a choice of green or yellow shirts. They can get blue, red, or silver pants. Name all of the uniform combinations they have to choose from.

2. Explain how you solved the problem.

____

____

____

3. Suppose the team had the same choices for shirt color and pants color but they also had to choose black or white numbers for their shirts. Name all possible pants, shirt, and number color combinations.

4. How can you be sure that you included all possible combinations?

____

____

____

5. Which uniform would you choose? ______________________

Name ____

Movie Theater Math

1. Five children were in line to buy movie tickets. Brendan was next to Justin. Sam was behind Justin but in front of Al. Ray was in front of Brendan. Name the order in which they were standing from first in line to last in line.

   ____

   Explain how you solved this problem.

   ____

   ____

   ____

   ____

2. The movie theater had a special deal. The cost for admission, popcorn, and a soda was $8.75. Regular admission is $6.50. Soda is regularly sold for $1.75, and popcorn costs $2.25. How much did each boy save with the special deal?

   ____

   Explain how you solved the problem.

   ____

   ____

   ____

   ____

Name ____

About How Many?

1. About how many math books could you stack on top of each other for the stack to reach the ceiling of your classroom?

   ____

2. Write a plan for solving this problem without actually stacking books to the ceiling.

   ____
   ____
   ____
   ____
   ____
   ____
   ____

3. About how many words are on one page of a newspaper? ____________

4. Make a plan for solving this problem without actually counting all of the words on the page.

   ____
   ____
   ____
   ____
   ____
   ____
   ____

Name ____________________

Think About It

What was easy about today's math lesson?

What was hard about today's lesson?

Reproducible

Name ______________________________

Sum It Up

Write a summary of what you learned today in math class.

IN SUMMATION

What questions do you have about today's lesson?

I HAVE A QUESTION!

Name ____

Math for Today

Today I used math when . . .

Name ____

Important Numbers

Numbers are used to tell us many things. Find some numbers that give information about your state or country. You might include numbers that tell the size of the state or country, the number of people living there, or the average annual snowfall. Be sure to label each number fact on your list.

158,869
1850

14.77
32,666,550

Select two number facts from your list. Why are these numbers important? Who might need to know them?

Name ____

Interview—Math on the Job

Develop a list of interview questions that will help you find out how someone uses mathematics in his or her job. Be specific in your questions—does the person deal with money? Does measurement play a part in his or her job? If so, how?

TELL ME...

Using your list of questions, interview a family member or a family friend about the role of math in his or her job.

Name ____

Speech—Math on the Job

Use your interview questions and answers to write a speech describing to your classmates how math is important in that job.

Answer Key

Note: Explanations and examples for open-ended questions will vary. The answers supplied are guidelines, highlighting key points. To conserve space, the phrase *Answers will vary* is not always repeated.

NUMERATION

Round It, page 8

1. 4,300. Explanations will vary but should mention looking to the right of the place to which you are rounding; if the digit is 5 or more, round up; if it is less than 5, keep the digit the same.
2. 7,000. Explanations will vary.
3. 23,000. Explanations will vary.

Write It Out, page 9

1. a. Sixty-five thousand, three hundred twelve
   b. Four hundred thirty-six million, two hundred seven thousand, four hundred
   c. Two million, seven hundred fifty-one thousand, fourteen
   d. Seven hundred fifty thousand, six hundred three
   e. Fifty million, three hundred eighty-one thousand, one hundred twenty-nine
   f. Six hundred twenty-one thousand, four hundred seventy-three
2. 600,000 + 20,000 + 1,000 + 400 + 70 + 3
3. Explanations will vary but should mention writing the number as the sum of the place values of the digits (i.e., 231 = 200 + 30 + 1).

Prime or Composite? page 10

1. A prime number is a number greater than 1 that has only two factors, 1 and itself.
2. Examples will vary.
3. A composite number has more than two factors.
4. Examples will vary.
5. Prime: 2, 3, 5, 7, 11, 13, 17, 19
   Composite: 4, 6, 8, 9, 10, 12, 14, 15, 16, 18, 20
6. Explanations will vary but might mention the number of factors as a way to determine where to place each number.

Puzzling Patterns, page 11

1. 4, 8, 16, 32, 64, 128, 256 . . .
   Pattern: doubling; multiplying by two
2. 3, 15, 75, 375, 1,875, 9,375, 46,875 . . .
   Pattern: multiplying by five
3. 2, 5, 9, 14, 20, 27, 35 . . .
   Pattern: + 3, + 4, + 5, + 6 . . . or adding one more each time
4. Original patterns and descriptions will vary.

Estimates Are OK, page 12

Answers will vary.

WHOLE NUMBERS

Multiples and Factors, page 13

1. A multiple is the product of a whole number and any other whole number.
2. Answers may include 7, 14, 28, 35, 42, 49, 56, 63, 70, 77, and 84.
3. Factors are the numbers that are multiplied to get a product.
4. 1, 2, 4, 8, 16, 32
5. Explanations will vary.

Find the Average, page 14

1. 15
2. To find the average, you add the books read by each person and then divide by the number of people.
3. Answers will vary.

My Own Story Problems, page 15

Original problems and solutions will vary but should match the equations.

Multiplication Mysteries, page 16

1. Possible diagram:

```
oooooo     oooo
oooooo     oooo
oooooo     oooo
oooooo     oooo
           oooo
           oooo
```

2. Explanations will vary but might mention that the 0 could represent the number of groups (0 groups of 6 = 0) or the number in a group (6 groups of 0 = 0).
3. No. Explanations will vary but may include one or more examples to support the answer.

Grow a Factor Tree, page 17

1. 50 → 5, 10; 10 → 2, 5
2. Answers will vary.
3. No. Explanations will vary but should include examples to support the argument.

Exponents and Factors, page 18

1.

2. Exponents help shorten descriptions of prime factors (e.g., the prime factors of 64 are 2 x 2 x 2 x 2 x 2 x 2, or 2^6.)
3. $2^3 = 2 \times 2 \times 2 = 8$

Exponents and Factors, page 18 continued

4. $3^2 \times 2^3 = 72$. Explanations will vary but should mention that 3^2 is 3 x 3 (9), 2^3 is 2 x 2 x 2 (8), and 9 x 8 = 72.

ASAP, Find the GCF and LCM! page 19

1. The GCF is the largest number that is a factor of each of two or more numbers.
2. 8 is the largest number that is a factor of both 24 and 32.
3. 6; 5; 6
4. The LCM is the smallest number other than 0 that is a multiple of each of two or more numbers.
5. The LCM of 9 and 6 is 18, the smallest number that is a multiple of both 9 and 6.
6. 24; 60; 30

What's Happening? page 20

1. 12. Each number on the left is multiplied by three, or tripled, to get the number on the right.
2. 25. Each number on the left is multiplied by itself, or squared, to get the number on the right.
3. Original tables and rules will vary.

GEOMETRY

Three Terrific Triangles, page 21

1. *Isosceles triangle:* a triangle with two equal sides and two equal angles opposite those sides.
   Equilateral triangle: a triangle with three equal sides and three equal angles.
   Scalene triangle: a triangle with no equal sides or angles.
2. Drawings should accurately represent each type of triangle.

Circle Talk, page 22

1. A chord is a line segment that connects two points on a circle. A diameter is a chord that runs through the center of the circle. The radius is a line segment from the center of the circle to any point on the circle. The center of a circle is the point in the circle that is the same distance from all points on the circle.
2. 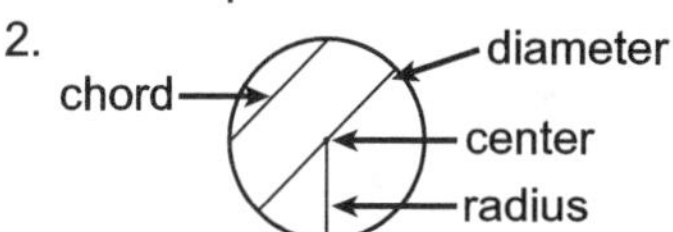

3. The radius is half of the diameter. The diameter is twice the distance of the radius.
4. The diameter is a chord that goes through the center of the circle.

Similar or Congruent? page 23

1. Similar figures have the same shape, just like congruent figures. Similar figures are not necessarily the same size, but congruent figures are.
2. Diagrams will vary.

What's Your Angle? page 24

1. *Acute angle:* an angle that measures less than 90 degrees (a right angle).
   Obtuse angle: an angle that measures more than 90 degrees (a right angle) but less than 180 degrees.
   Right angle: an angle that measures 90 degrees.
2. Drawings will vary but should be accurate.

All About Angles, page 25

1. Drawings will vary but should be accurate.
2. Explanations will vary but should mention that if the angle (vertex) of the triangle looks greater than that of a right triangle, then its measure is greater than 90 degrees.
3. A protractor
4. Angle 1: 45 degrees; Angle 2: 120 degrees
5. Explanations will vary but should include descriptions similar to the following: *I know if the angle is larger or smaller than 90 degrees by the way it looks. I chose the number based on this.*

Six Solid Shapes, page 26

1. Triangular prism: 5 flat faces, 9 edges, 6 vertices
   Square pyramid: 5 flat faces, 8 edges, 5 vertices
2. A rectangular prism has 6 flat faces, 12 straight edges, and 8 vertices.
3. A cylinder has 2 curved edges, 1 curved face, and 2 flat faces.
4. Answers will vary.

Symmetry, page 27

1. Yes. Explanations will vary but might mention that if you fold the figure, one part fits exactly over the other.

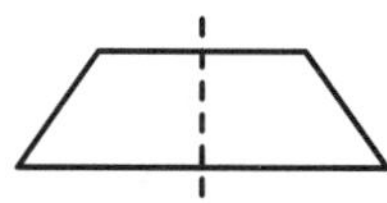

2. No. Explanations will vary but might mention that there is no way to fold this figure so that one part fits exactly over the other.
3. Answers and drawings will vary but should be accurate.

MEASUREMENT

How Much Should You Buy? page 28

1. 6 dozen eggs. Explanations will vary but should mention that dividing the total by 12 (eggs in a dozen). Explanations should include that if you need a few extra eggs, you will need to buy another dozen.
2. 4 yards of ribbon. Explanations will vary but should mention dividing the total by 3 (feet in a yard) and then adding another yard if more ribbon footage is needed.

Nearest Dollar, page 29

1. $1.00 $4.00
   $2.00 $6.00
   $1.00 $3.00
   $7.00 $9.00
2. $33.00
3. Directions will vary but might mention looking at the digit to the right of the decimal point to decide if the dollar amount should be rounded up or stay the same.
4. $1.50. Explanations will vary but may say that $1.49 would be rounded to $1.00 and $1.50 would be rounded to $2.00.

Coin Combinations, page 30

1. 3 coins: 1 quarter, 2 pennies. Explanations will vary but may show that other coin combinations would use more coins.
2. 4 coins: 1 quarter, 2 dimes, 1 penny.
3. 6 coins: 1 half dollar, 1 dime, 1 nickel, 3 pennies.
4. 5 coins: 1 half dollar, 1 quarter, 1 nickel, 2 pennies.
5. 6 coins: 1 dollar, 1 half dollar, 1 quarter, 2 dimes, 1 penny.
6. Tips will vary but may include beginning with the largest possible coin and then moving to the next largest.

Sleeping or Studying? page 31

1. Estimates and explanations will vary but might mention the hours of sleep each night x 7 nights or the hours on school nights x 5 nights plus the hours on weekend nights x 2 nights.
2. You will need to know the number of hours you spend in school each week.
3. Answers and student comments will vary.

Inside and Around, page 32

1. Area is the number of square units needed to cover a region. You find the area by counting squares or by multiplying the length times the width for rectangles.
2. Perimeter is the distance around a polygon. You find the perimeter of a rectangle by measuring the sides and adding the measurements together.
3. No. Explanations will vary but could include examples such as the following: A 12 unit by 2 unit figure has a perimeter of 28 units, but a 6 unit by 4 unit figure has a perimeter of 20 units.
4. Answers will vary and may include diagrams.

Picnic Problem, page 33

1. Each person will get 1 pint of soda, a 4" x 6" piece of pizza (or other reasonable division), 4 oz. of potato chips, 12 grapes, and $1\frac{1}{2}$ brownies.
2. Justifications will vary, but the plan should be fair.

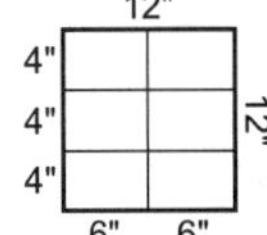

Do You Have Enough? page 34

1. No. You need 90 yards and only have 80 yards.
2. Yes. You need 180 square feet and have 200 square feet.
3. No. You need 108 square feet and only have 100 square feet.

Time to Swim, page 35

1. 3:15 p.m. Explanations will vary but should show an understanding of elapsed time.
2. 1 hour and 25 minutes. Explanations will vary.
3. 5:05
4. Original problems and solutions will vary.

RATIONAL NUMBERS

Fraction Action, page 36

Drawings will vary but should accurately represent the fractions.

Fishy Fractions, page 37

1. 16 students. Divide 24 students by 3 = 8, then multiply 8 x 2 = 16.
2. a. 8; b. 12; c. 16; d. 9; e. 4; f. 14; g. 15.
3. 8 (H); 12 (L); 16 (P); 9 (I); 4 (D); 14 (N); 15 (O). Students' favorite: DOLPHIN.

Equivalent Fractions, page 38

1. Equivalent fractions are fractions that name the same number.
2. Fractions will vary but may include $\frac{4}{6}$, $\frac{6}{9}$, $\frac{8}{12}$, and $\frac{10}{15}$.
3. Fractions will vary but may include $\frac{8}{10}$, $\frac{12}{15}$, $\frac{16}{20}$, and $\frac{20}{25}$.
4. Directions will vary but should mention multiplying the numerator and denominator by the same number.

Sale! page 39

1. Shirt: $11.25
   Jeans: $17.50
   Gloves: $4.50
   Hat: $6.30
   Sandals: $7.85
   Athletic shoes: $18.20
2. You find the sale prices by multiplying by $\frac{1}{2}$ or dividing by 2.
3. Answers will vary.

Challenge: Answers and explanations will vary.

Adding Fractions, page 40

1. a. $\frac{6}{9}$ or $\frac{2}{3}$; b. $\frac{10}{21}$; c. $\frac{8}{12}$ or $\frac{2}{3}$; d. $\frac{5}{18}$
2. Directions will vary but should mention adding the numerators and keeping the common denominator. Students may mention reducing the fraction to lowest terms as a final step.
3. Directions should be similar to those in Question 2, except that students will first need to identify a common denominator and then find equivalent fractions with that denominator for one or both of the equivalent fractions.

Convince Me, page 41

Answers will vary.

It's Just Not Proper! page 42

1. An improper fraction is a fraction in which the numerator is greater than or equal to the denominator.
2. a. $1\frac{5}{7}$ d. $3\frac{3}{4}$
   b. $2\frac{2}{6}$ or $2\frac{1}{3}$ e. $4\frac{1}{6}$
   c. $2\frac{5}{8}$
3. First, divide the numerator by the denominator to find the whole number. Then, use the remainder as the numerator of the new fraction and use the original denominator as the denominator. Students may use examples to explain the process.

Ready, Set, Reduce! page 43

1. No. $\frac{6}{10}$ is equivalent to $\frac{3}{5}$, not $\frac{2}{5}$. Explanations may include diagrams.
2. Yes. $\frac{6}{9}$ is equivalent to $\frac{2}{3}$. Explanations may include diagrams.
3. a. $\frac{1}{3}$ d. $\frac{2}{5}$
   b. $\frac{1}{4}$ e. $\frac{3}{4}$
   c. $\frac{1}{5}$ f. $\frac{3}{5}$
4. Explanations will vary but should mention dividing both the numerator and denominator by the same number until the fraction can't be reduced further. In lowest terms, $\frac{4}{24}$ is $\frac{1}{6}$.

Decimal Patterns, page 44

1. 4.5, 5.1, 5.7
   Pattern: Add six tenths to each number.

Decimal Patterns, page 44 continued

2. 9, 10.5, 12
   Pattern: Add 1.5 to each number.
3. 4.61, 4.63, 4.65
   Pattern: Add two hundredths to each number.
4. Original patterns and descriptions will vary.

Round the Jumps, page 45

1. Jean 66
   Pat 75
   Terrell 62
   Bobby 84
   Kathleen 83
   Carol 70
   Carlos 72
   Michael 72
2. Ties could be decided by looking at the decimals before they were rounded, or another reasonable answer.
3. a. Bobby e. Michael
   b. Kathleen f. Carol
   c. Pat g. Jean
   d. Carlos h. Terrell
4. Explanations will vary, but should mention looking at the digit to the right of the decimal point to determine whether the whole number should be rounded up (the digit is 5 or more) or stay the same (4 or less).

Same Number, Different Name, page 46

1. 0.32; thirty-two hundredths
   0.6; six tenths
   0.53; fifty-three hundredths
   0.07; seven hundredths
2. Explanations will vary and may include diagrams.

Tricky Tenths and Hundredths, page 47

1. 2.14 is greater than 2.08 because 2.14 has one tenth and 2.08 has no tenths.
2. 7.5 is greater than 7.05 because 7.5 has five tenths and 7.05 has no tenths.
3. 2.04, 2.08, 2.48, 2.8, 2.84.
4. Tips will vary but may include looking at the whole numbers first, then at the tenths, then at the hundredths, and so on.

Percents to Ponder, page 48

1. A percent is a ratio that compares a number to one hundred. Percent means parts per hundred.
2. 5. Explanations will vary but might mention converting the percentage to a decimal (10% to 0.1) and multiplying it by the number of jelly beans (50) to get the number that are green (5).
3. a. 7; b. 40; c. 12; d. 9; e. 40
4. Answers will vary.

DATA ANALYSIS

The Best Graph, page 49

1. A line graph would be appropriate because it would show the trend over time.
2. A bar graph, pictograph, or circle graph would be appropriate. The circle graph would show the divisions of favorite cookies for the class as a whole. The bar and pictographs would display each distinct piece of data.
3. A bar graph or pictograph would be appropriate to display the distinct pieces of data.
4. Answers will vary, but there should be two parts to the data displayed.

Diving Data, page 50

1. Melissa 8.5
   Colleen 8.4
   Rita 8.3
   Megan 7.9
   Erica 7.7
2. If you threw out the high and low scores and then selected the winner based on the median score, the winner would still be Melissa, with a median score of 8.7. The other median scores (7.8, 8.6, 8.3, 7.9) were all less than that.

Flavor Graph, page 51

1. Graphs should accurately represent data.
2.–4. Answers will vary.

Ice Cream by the Hour, page 52

1. Graphs should accurately represent data.
2.–3. Answers will vary.

Favorite Cereals, page 53

1. The graph shows favorite cereals for adults and children.
2.–4. Answers will vary.

Carnival Coupons, page 54

1.

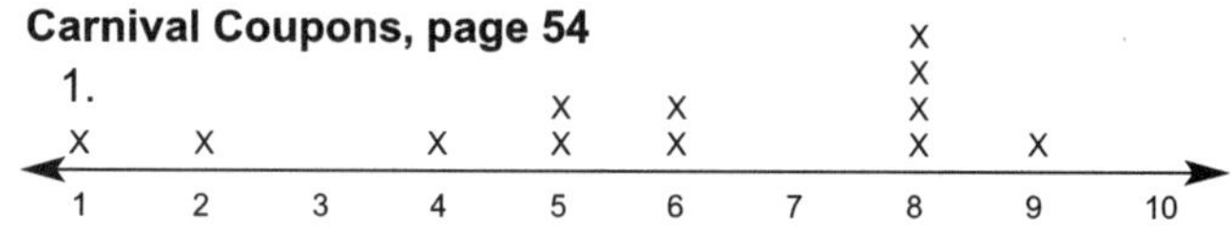

2. 9
3. 1
4. 8. Explanations will vary but should indicate that the range is the difference between the smallest and largest values.
5. 8. Explanations will vary but should indicate that the mode is the most frequently occurring number in a set of data.

Sweet Sales, page 55

1. 61 boxes. Explanations will vary but should represent the largest number on the plot.
2. 40 boxes. Explanations will vary but should represent the smallest number on the plot.
3. Estimates will vary but should be reasonable. Explanations will vary but should be based on the plot data.
4. 16. Explanations will vary.
5. 11. Explanations will vary.

Bicycle Prices, page 56

1. $35.00. The range represents the difference between the lowest cost and the highest cost. You figure it out by subtracting one from the other.
2. $114.00
3. $115.00
4. The mean is the average cost. The median is the middle cost (in this problem, it is the price that has three prices above and three below).
5. The mode is the most frequently repeated value.
6. $115.00

PROBABILITY

A Tree-mendous Diagram, page 57

1.–2.

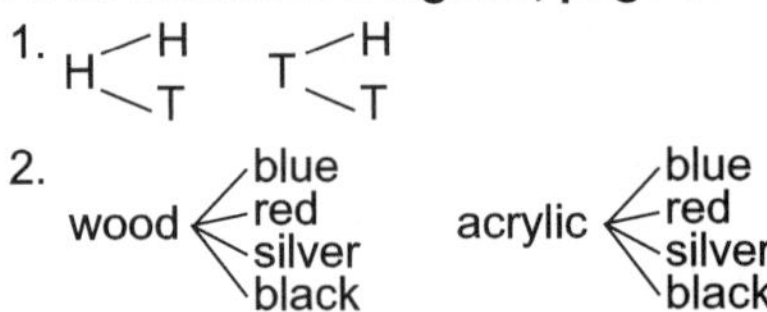

3. Explanations will vary but might mention keeping the data organized or exhausting one possibility before moving to another.

Equally Likely? page 58

1.–2. Answers will vary.

3. *Equally likely* means that outcomes have the same chance of happening.

Roll the Die page 59

1. $\frac{1}{6}$. Explanations will vary but should demonstrate knowledge that there is only one 3 and six possible outcomes.
2. $\frac{2}{6}$. Explanations will vary but should demonstrate knowledge that there are only two possibilities out of six.
3. $\frac{3}{6}$. Explanations will vary but should demonstrate knowledge that there are only three possibilities out of six.
4. Answers will vary.

Marble Probability, page 60

1. 5. Green, red, blue, yellow, orange
2. Green, because there are more green marbles in the bag than any other color
3. Yellow or orange, because there is only one of each
4. Black, purple, or any other color that is not in the bag
5. No. Explanations will vary but may indicate that likelihood is not the same as outcome.

PROBLEM SOLVING

What's Your Strategy? page 61

1. 16 posts. Explanations will vary. Drawing a picture or diagram is a typical strategy for solving this problem.
2. American League 15, National League 9. Explanations will vary. Guess, check, and revise is a typical strategy for solving this problem.

Playground Favorites, page 62

1. Gail: kickball
   José: jump rope
   Kelly: basketball
   Maria: tag
2. Explanations will vary.

Muffins Enough, page 63

1. Three batches, because there are 28 students. Two batches will give her 24 muffins, which is not enough.
2. 6 cups flour
   3 eggs
   3 cups chocolate chips
   $1\frac{1}{2}$ teaspoon cinnamon sugar
   $\frac{3}{4}$ cup sugar
   2 cups milk
   1 cup chopped nuts
3. Explanations will vary but should indicate tripling, multiplying by three, or adding the number three times.
4. Original problems and solutions will vary.

Please Explain, page 64

1. 8 students. Explanations will vary. Using logical reasoning and a Venn diagram is a typical way to solve this problem.
2. $65.50. Explanations will vary. Working backward is a typical strategy for solving this problem.

What a Racket! page 65

1. $36.21. Explanations will vary.
2. The Tennis Bargain Pack is a good deal because if you bought the items separately they would cost $44.18, which is more than the bargain price of $39.95.
3. The cost for all five items is $74.63 if you buy the Bargain Pack and the other two items.

The Riddler, page 66

1. 36
2. 21
3. 27
4. Tips will vary but may include writing down the numbers and crossing off those eliminated.
5. Original riddles will vary.
6. Answers will vary.

Color Combos, page 67

1. Students may make a list or tree diagram to determine the combinations.
2. Explanations will vary but may include making an organized list or a tree diagram.

green: blue, red, silver
yellow: blue, red, silver

3.

4. Explanations will vary, but students should have proceeded in an organized way to be sure that all possibilities have been found.
5. Answers will vary.

Movie Theater Math, page 68

1. Ray, Brendan, Justin, Sam, Al. Explanations will vary. Drawing a diagram is a typical strategy for solving this problem.
2. $1.75. Explanations will vary but should include a comparison of the regular cost of $10.50 and the special deal cost of $8.75.

About How Many? page 69

1. Answers will vary.
2. Plans will vary but may include checking the height of a few math books and then estimating.
3. Answers will vary.
4. Plans will vary but may include checking the number of words in a section of the page (sampling) and then estimating.

REFLECTIONS

Pages 70–76

Answers will vary.